ALL THINGS CHICKENS FOR KIDS

FILLED WITH PLENTY OF FACTS, PHOTOS, AND FUN TO LEARN ALL ABOUT CHICKENS

ANIMAL READS

WWW.ANIMALREADS.COM

THIS BOOK BELONGS TO...

_____

_____

WWW.ANIMALREADS.COM

CONTENTS

An Introduction to Chickens	1
Characteristics and Appearance	7
Many Kinds of Chickens	17
A History of Chickens	39
Where do Chickens Live?	45
The Life Cycle of a Chicken	53
Awesome Facts About Chickens & Chicken Talk	65
Thank You!	73

AN INTRODUCTION TO CHICKENS

We bet if we asked you which kind of bird is the most common in the world, we might get a few different answers. You might say the crow is the most common. Maybe someone would say a robin. But actually, the bird with the largest population in the world is the chicken!

That's right. **There are over 23 billion chickens in the world today!** This is even more amazing when you realize there are only 7.7 billion or so people on the planet. *That means there are around 3 chickens to every 1 person living on earth today.* If chickens ever decided to take over, **we'd be in big trouble!**

*Thankfully, chickens don't seem to have any plans for world domination right now, so we think we're all safe... **or are we???***

No other domesticated animal even comes close to the number of chickens. If you added up all of the cows, pigs, dogs, and cats on the planet, they would only come to 3.5 billion animals. At 23 billion, chickens easily outpace them all as the domestic animal with the largest number.

WHAT IS A CHICKEN?

Chickens are birds that are part of the jungle fowl species. The scientific Latin name for chicken is *Gallus gallus domesticus*. Can you hear the word "*domestic*" in that last word?

That means chickens are a domesticated animal, which is a fancy way of saying they have been bred over the years to live with and help people. Unlike wild birds, chickens are relatively tame, easily managed by people, and have been bred to have qualities people find helpful.

Another word you may have heard when talking about chickens is "*poultry*." Poultry is what farmers and food producers call birds raised for meat, eggs, or feathers. The term poultry refers to chickens, ducks, geese, turkeys, and guinea fowl.

CHARACTERISTICS AND APPEARANCE

␣t's hard to mistake a chicken! Whether or not you have ever been to a farm in real life, most of us have learned about chickens from the time we could first look at a barnyard book. Few birds have that same rounded body, skinny legs, and fluffy feathers.

Chickens have a comb on their head that is often red in color, but that can change depending on the breed. Most people know that roosters have a comb, but hens do as well, although a rooster's comb is larger. Chickens also have wattles, which are two red flaps that hang from the top of their beak.

Like other birds, chickens have a very hard beak. They use this beak to peck and eat. Their beaks continue to grow so that they are never worn down. On the beak, chickens have nostrils for breathing. Chickens also use their beak for drinking. They do this by putting their beaks into the water, holding a small amount, and then tipping their heads back to let the water flow into their mouths.

Chickens walk on 2 legs. Since they also move their heads when they walk, chickens have a kind of strut when they move. They are too heavy to fly very much, but chickens can flap their wings and get a few feet off the ground.

Chickens are also able to soar and glide several feet. Some lighter breeds can flap up into low tree branches. If given the opportunity, chickens like to sleep in trees or at least up off the ground.

This characteristic seems to be a hold-over from their wild days. Roosting in a tree is safer than sleeping on the ground, where a chicken is more vulnerable to predators creeping around at night.

Chickens are very in tune with the seasons and the light. When the sun comes up, roosters crow. When the sun goes down, the chickens return to the safety of their coop for the night, and the flock will all sleep together.

Chickens do not like to live alone. A single, solitary chicken will be very sad and lonely. Chickens are very social and love to live in a flock of at least 3 chickens. Many of the sounds chickens make are ways they communicate within their flock. *Did you know that chickens can make 24 different kinds of sounds?* **It's true.**

WHAT DO CHICKENS EAT?

If you asked the average person what chickens eat, you might get answers like this: *grain, corn, plants.* And none of those answers would be wrong! Chickens **do** eat all of those things.

But most people may mistakenly believe that chickens are herbivores and that they only eat a vegetarian, plant-based diet. *But that is very far from the truth!*

Chickens, like most people, are *omnivores*. That means they do eat plants but also eat meat as well. You may be thinking, *"What? How do* *chickens eat meat?"* After all, aren't chickens smaller than most meat animals? And the thought of a chicken eating a hamburger is pretty silly.

While it's true that chickens don't eat pigs and cows, chickens *do* eat bugs. **They eat a lot of bugs!**

Chickens love to eat slugs, worms, and almost any bug they can get their beaks on provided it doesn't taste bad to them. Chickens have lightening fast reflexes and sharp eyesight! They can spot a tiny little critter and peck it up before you even know what's happening. In fact, some of the most famous chicken behavior, like scratching at the ground and pecking, is all about finding bugs. People who have backyard chickens benefit from all that hunting and pecking too. Chickens love to eat ticks and other bugs that humans consider to be pests. Having free-range chickens can greatly decrease the population of unwanted bugs in an area.

Chickens don't stop at bugs, though. Mice, small snakes, and tiny lizards are all fair game to chickens as well!

Chickens also love to eat food waste. Most chicken owners keep a container in their kitchen for chicken scraps. *Didn't finish that slice of pizza?* Stick it in the chicken bucket. *Did your cereal get a little too mushy, and you just can't finish it?* The chickens will love it! This is another plus to having backyard chickens—less waste in the trash can. **So, maybe chickens do eat hamburgers after all!**

MANY KINDS OF CHICKENS

There are several hundred different breeds of chickens in the world today! Some chickens look like wild, puffy-cheeked birds, and some look like plump, docile farmyard animals. Chickens can be white, black, red, and almost any other color. *There are even chickens that are lavender!*

All chickens can be divided into 3 groups: **laying** breeds, **meat** breeds, and **fancy/show** breeds. Let's take a look at some of the most popular species in each of these groups.

Laying Breeds

Laying breeds are chickens that have been bred over the years to have the best egg production. These days, a good laying hen that is fed well can lay up to almost 300 eggs a year. In the early 1900s, a hen who laid 125 eggs a year was considered to be a good layer! With better food and breeding, the number of eggs have increased.

So, what are the most popular laying breeds around today? Let's take a look!

WHITE LEGHORN

White Leghorns are your typical farmyard chicken. They are large and white, big surprise! They also lay white eggs. Most of the eggs in the supermarket are probably laid by white leghorns, as many of the big commercial egg producers use this breed of chicken. There is a reason for that! These chickens are hardy, do well in a pen, and can lay 280 to 300 eggs yearly.

RHODE ISLAND RED

Another very popular chicken for egg production is the Rhode Island Red. This breed is a deep red color and originated from Rhode Island in the U.S. As you can see, chicken breed names tend to be very practical and describe unique characteristics of that breed, like what it looks like or where it is from originally.

These chickens are hardy as well, which means they don't get sick very easily. They lay an impressive 260 eggs a year. Rhode Island Reds are also good at free-ranging or foraging. That makes them an excellent choice for backyard chickens or for small farms that can let the chickens forage around and find some of their own food.

Although some breeds are better at this, they still need access to chicken food as well to make sure they get a balanced diet and to ensure they can keep producing a large number of eggs. **It takes a lot of energy to lay an egg!** If the chicken can't get enough food, it will start to lay fewer eggs.

AMERAUCANA

Ameraucanas are a breed that is well-loved for their colored eggs. That's right! *These chickens lay eggs that are light blue, green, or turquoise.* They are only 1 of 5 chicken breeds that lay colored eggs (*not just white, tan, or brown*).

One hen will have a particular color and continue to lay that color her entire life. Because of this neat trait, ameraucanas are a popular breed and are even nicknamed "*Easter Eggers.*" They lay around 250 eggs a year and have a wilder appearance with puffy, feathered cheeks and sleeker bodies. Developed from the South American araucana breed, ameraucanas are slightly less friendly and can fly better and roost in low branches of trees.

BUFF ORPINGTON

The buff orpington is a big beautiful chicken that makes a great addition to any backyard coop or small hobby farm. These chickens are a friendly and fluffy breed that make great pets as well. While they don't lay as well as some other breeds at only 150-200 eggs a year, they are sweet-natured and docile birds that do well in a coop and are good for kids. Buff orpingtons are a "buff" orange/tan color, but they also come in other varieties such as blue/gray, black, white, chocolate, lavender, red, and many different shades!

Another great thing about this breed is that it is a heritage breed. That means it is a breed that has been around a long time and has a history of being raised by homesteaders and farmers. Some small farms today like to raise heritage breeds to continue in that tradition and to ensure these breeds aren't lost just because they aren't raised by commercial chicken farms. Since homesteaders from long ago needed chickens that could be good for both meat and eggs, many heritage breeds fall into a category we call "*dual-purpose breeds.*" Buff orpingtons are a dual-purpose breed that can be raised for their eggs but also for their meat.

Meat Breeds

So far, we have mainly discussed chickens as egg producers, but if you've ever had a chicken sandwich or a piece of chicken with your warm meals, you know chickens are also raised for meat. It is sad to realize that the meat you eat was once a chicken or another farm animal. Still, farming and using animal products have helped humans evolve into what we are today.

It is important to try and support small and large farmers who raise chickens ethically and kindly. We can all do this by eating healthy balanced meals and by buying organic or free-range meat and eggs. Meat breeds are developed to grow quickly, have a good weight, and have lots of meat on their bodies.

Let's look at a few breeds that are popular with chicken producers and also a few heritage breeds.

CORNISH CROSS

The Cornish cross breed is the most common breed found in U.S. grocery stores today. They are large white chickens that have been developed to grow very fast. They are categorized as "*rapid*" growing chicken. They have large chests, which give off more breast meat when they are processed. These chickens have been bred to go from tiny chicks to mature chickens in only 6 weeks. The poultry industry has developed this breed to get the most meat in the least amount of time with the least amount of food. This is a good system if your goal is to make the most money possible from your chicken farm. However, many people find the rapid growth of this breed to be unnatural and even inhumane. Because the Cornish cross has such a heavy, meaty body, it is difficult for the birds to move around. If they are not butchered at the 6 week mark, they will quickly get too big for their legs and heart to support themselves. For this reason, many small farms and homesteads who want to raise their own meat humanely and ethically don't raise Cornish cross chickens.

RANGER

There is an alternative to the Cornish cross for farmers who still want to raise a quick-growing chicken but don't want to do so in an unethical way. *Ranger chickens are also fast-growing, but their growth doesn't outpace their own body's ability to support itself.* This breed is also a large chicken but has a slightly sweeter taste than the meat you are probably used to. Rangers can be tri-colored or red and take about 9 to 11 weeks to grow to 5 or 6 pounds.

JERSEY GIANT

The Jersey giant is a huge chicken! And, like you probably guessed, this breed produces a lot of meat. Unlike the other chicken in this group, however, Jersey giants take longer to grow. Instead of a matter of weeks like the other 2 breeds we mentioned, Jersey giants can take anywhere from 8-12 months to mature. That's right, months! One advantage to slow-growing breeds is the flavor! Jersey giants have a rich, full flavor and are quite tasty. Another plus to this heritage breed is that they also lay around 200 eggs a year, which is not bad at all for a meat breed. So, if you aren't in a hurry and care about preserving heritage breeds and you also like excellent meat, Jersey giants may be a good choice.

Fancy/Show Breeds

Let's face it, not all chickens are just bred for eggs or meat. Many people in the United States and all over the world breed chickens to show them in chicken shows. These people show chickens as a hobby and hope to win prizes and ribbons for showing the best-looking chicken of that breed. These fancy breeds have been developed to look beautiful or unusual.

Have you ever seen a chicken with feathers that go down to its feet? Ever seen a chicken with a plume of dark feathers so large on its head that it looks like it's wearing a hat? If you have, you were probably looking at a fancy breed. So, if you're in the market to have the most unique and beautiful chicken on the block, pull up a chair. **Nothing is more striking in the chicken world than these fancy feathered friends!**

SILKIE

Silkie chickens first originated in China long ago. Marco Polo, the famous European explorer who traveled to China, wrote about a fuzzy chicken that he encountered on his journey... Silkies. Silkie chickens are perhaps best known for their unusual feathers, which feel more like fuzz or silk than regular feathers. They are a favorite of fancy chicken enthusiasts because they are not only beautiful and amazingly soft, but they also have a great *temperament*. The word temperament means their attitude and how they act overall.

Silkies are known for being very sweet, calm, and easygoing. They are also great mothers! When a hen decides to "*go broody*," it means they sit on the eggs to try and hatch out baby chicks. Some breeds don't have very strong mothering tendencies anymore.

After all, most chicks are hatched out in incubators these days. Incubators are small heated cages that mimic a mother hen sitting on the eggs. Eggs must be kept warm to develop and hatch. Silkies are often used in place of an incubator and are used to hatch out the eggs of other less broody breeds. Silkies are bred mainly for showing and for pets.

COCHIN

Cochin chickens also have feathers that grow all the way down to cover their feet. However, unlike Silkies, Cochins have yellow skin, not black. First brought over to Europe and North America in the 1840s and 1850s, Cochins became very popular for their beautiful full feathers. These large birds come in various colors and are also good at hatching other chickens' eggs due to their broody nature.

However, although they are large birds, Cochins have not been developed for meat quality, so they do not make a good meat breed. However, don't let their giant size fool you. Cochins are sometimes called "*gentle giants.*" They are known for being easy to handle and having a calm temperament.

POLISH

Another beautiful and unusual fancy breed is the Polish chicken. These chickens look as if they have fancy feathered hats or wild hairdos. The Polish chicken has a large crest of feathers on the top of its head that splay out in all directions. They also have a smaller comb and wattles compared to other breeds. As they are a very old breed, not much is known about their origins, although they are thought to have originated in the Netherlands.

Paintings from the 1400s show chickens that look very similar to Polish chickens. As their crested feathers can make it harder for them to see, this breed is sometimes more timid and fearful and less easygoing than other fancy breeds.

THE PLOT CHICKENS!

A HISTORY OF CHICKENS

Have you ever watched a chicken strut across a farmyard, catch sight of a piece of grain out of the corner of its eye, and then attack? Chickens have amazingly fast reflexes and incredible eyesight.

If you look close enough and study them, you might even start to think chickens look a little like dinosaurs.

Seriously!

It isn't hard to picture chickens roaming the earth like tiny velociraptors.

There's a reason that chickens remind us of the prehistoric past. It turns out the connection between chickens and dinosaurs may not be farfetched at all!

Scientists have long wondered if dinosaurs and birds might share more of a connection than was first thought. In 2003, a T-Rex fossil was found with some blood vessels and tissue still on it. DNA was able to be taken from this preserved tissue, and researchers were able to make the DNA sequence for a T-Rex. This Dino DNA was then compared to different bird species. *Out of all the birds, **chicken DNA was the closest to the di-***

nosaur! Turkey DNA was also close to the DNA of the T-Rex.

There are other connections between dinosaurs and birds as well. A prehistoric bird dinosaur called the Archaeopteryx was a close relative to Velociraptors and the T-Rex. The Archaeopteryx flew, had feathers, and even a brain similar to today's birds.

Over tens of millions of years, one dinosaur group seems to have evolved into birds. Some 18,000 different kinds or species of birds exist today.

Modern-day chickens come from a species of wild jungle fowl in Asia.

Just a little over 2,000 years ago, people started to keep chickens for eggs and meat. *Today, it's hard to imagine a farm without chickens!*

HOW DO **CHICKENS** STAY FIT?

They <u>**EGGS**</u>-ercise!

WHERE DO CHICKENS LIVE?

Since chickens are domestic animals, they live everywhere people do!

Some chickens live on small farms and free-range all day for their food and enjoyment. These chickens live an ideal life of getting to be on the ground, scratching, pecking for bugs, flying about, and getting into chicken squabbles with each other.

When they are tired, chickens rest together in the shade of a tree or under a porch. They roll in the dust to coat their feathers and keep pests like fleas or lice off of themselves.

You may wonder how farmers gather all the chickens back to their coop at night. Chickens naturally return to the same place to roost each night. As the sun sets, free-range chickens start to make their way back to their coop. If they have poles or branches in their coop, chickens prefer to roost there and perch for the night. Once it is dark, chickens will sleep. In fact, if you are ever holding a chicken and want it to calm down, all you have to do is cover its head with a towel or your hand. The chicken will see it is dark and go into a sleepy state.

Raising free-range chickens may sound like the best option, and in many ways, it is! It is the most natural for chickens and offers them lots of opportunities to do all kinds of chicken things, like hunting and scratching around. However, the downside to raising chickens free-range is that it is more dangerous.

Predators would love nothing more than to sneak up on a chicken who is happily out pecking and scratching. Foxes, opossums, raccoons, and hawks are just a few of the predators that prey on chickens. And don't forget the sweet predator you may have living in your very own home—dogs.

That's right! Dogs, even your sweet golden retriever, have a strong prey drive. The flapping happy antics of chickens seem to kick the prey drive into high gear for many dogs.

Another option for free-ranging is raising chickens in a pen or coop. These chickens still have a yard area to flap around in, but they are protected from predators by a fence.

In places with lots of predators, coops may need to be completely secured and covered with chicken wire walls, ceilings, and locked doors. Raccoons, with their little hands, are extremely good at opening doors and simple latches if they want to.

While some chickens live free-range or in a secure pen/coop, most chickens in the world live in factory farm environments. These are large-scale operations whose goal is to make as much money as possible for as little cost. These chickens live their whole lives indoors in large chicken sheds.

They do not get to go out on the grass or see the outdoors or the sunshine. Egg layers live in tiny cages crowded into rows with other chickens. Sadly, these chickens live stressed lives and don't get to do any of the "*chicken*" behaviors that their free-range counterparts get to experience.

Whenever possible, choosing to support egg and meat producers that raise chickens in a free-range environment is a good idea, both for the quality of the eggs and meat, and for the quality of life given to the chickens.

WHAT IS A GREAT AFTERNOON ACTIVITY FOR CHICKENS?

A <u>PECK</u>-nic!

THE LIFE CYCLE OF A CHICKEN

Let's take a moment to explore the life cycle of a chicken. From egg to a grandma or grandpa age chicken!

FROM EGG TO CHICK

As you probably know, before you can have a chicken, **you need an egg!** But you can't just go into your fridge and grab any old egg. To raise a chick, you need a fertilized egg. *But how does an egg become fertilized?* Eggs begin first as a yolk inside a hen. The yolk is the yellow part of the egg. The yolk stays inside a hen's oviduct, which is a kind of tunnel for eggs to form inside the hen.

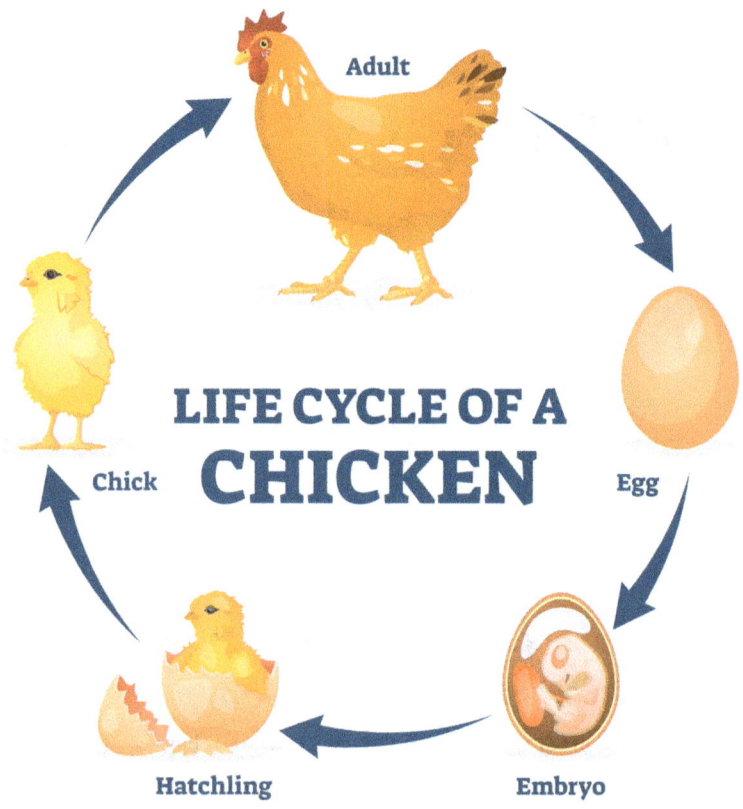

The yolk becomes fertilized when an adult male chicken, a rooster, mates with an adult female chicken, a hen. The now fertile yolk continues to pass through the oviduct. Within about a day, the yolk will be covered in a membrane and other layers, which become the egg white.

At the end of the oviduct, the egg will get a shell that is made of calcium. Then the hen will lay the egg in a nest she made in straw or other bedding. Yolks that are not fertilized go through this same process and also become eggs, only they can never develop into chicks.

That isn't the end of the story for our egg. It isn't magically going to hatch just yet!

Once the egg is laid, the egg must be kept warm and at the right temperature and humidity to grow into a chick and hatch. This can either be done one of two ways.

The first way for an egg to stay warm enough is by a broody hen sitting on it. A broody hen is a hen whose instincts make her want to sit on a group of eggs and hatch them out. She will get up only to eat and drink but will spend most of the time sitting on the eggs.

The second way an egg can be hatched is in an incubator. An incubator is a plastic cage that keeps the eggs at the right temperature and humidity. Some fancy incubators even turn the eggs over a couple times a day. If a hen is sitting on eggs, she will turn the eggs too.

If the egg is not kept warm or if it is put in the fridge, it will not develop into a chick. Fertilized eggs can be eaten the same as unfertilized eggs and don't taste any differently.

To help you remember the process of getting a chick, here is a simple equation:

Fertilized egg + warmth + 21 days = a chick

Fertilized egg + no warmth + 21 days = no chick

Unfertilized egg + warmth + 21 days = no chick

As you can see, you need the right combination of a fertilized egg **and** a warm environment of the right temperature to hatch out a chick. A warm fertilized egg will start to develop into an embryo. Amazingly, just 21 days later, a fully-formed chick will peck its way out of the shell!

FROM BABY CHICK TO TEENAGER PULLET

Just like baby humans, baby chicks are fragile and need a lot of care. One difference is that baby chicks can begin to eat and digest solid food just a day or 2 after hatching. They also can walk, peep, and clean themselves.

As the baby chicks mature, they enjoy jumping on things like cardboard tubes, the edge of their food or water dish, and each other! Baby chicks often knock water dishes over and poop in their food. They aren't too concerned about making a mess.

This jumping and fluttering behavior helps them get stronger and practice flying. They will need to master these skills when they are older to perch at night for sleep or to get away quickly from predators.

A few weeks into life and the chicks will start to grow feathers over their downy fluff. They will also begin to grow combs and wattles. At this point, it is sometimes possible to tell the sex of the chicks as they turn into **pullets** (*young hens*) or **cockerels** (*young roosters*). Cockerels will start to have a larger comb and wattles. Sometimes they will develop the "*cocky*" and bossy attitude of a rooster as well.

MATURING INTO A FULLY-FUNCTIONAL EGG-LAYING HEN OR CROWING ROOSTER

A hen is considered mature and an adult when it starts laying eggs. This can be anytime after 20 weeks of age. Some chickens continue to grow in size up to 1 year old. A mature rooster will start to crow and will show an interest in leading its flock of hens and mating.

However, roosters do a lot more than crowing and mating. Roosters provide the hens with a feeling of security. Mature roosters are bold and brave. They have spurs on the backs of their legs with a sharp claw on each spur.

If necessary, a rooster will fight another animal, even a larger one, to protect his flock. He will die trying to protect his hens if necessary.

Chickens have a **hierarchical** flock, which means that they have a "*pecking order.*" In other words, every chicken knows where it stands in the group.

Some chickens fall at the bottom of the order, and they can get bossed around and even bullied or pecked. Other chickens are near the top of the order and enjoy the best sleeping places and choice of foods. The rooster is at the very top of the group. But the rooster, like we said earlier, takes this leadership seriously.

A good rooster will cluck to call his hens to food, but he won't eat right away to make sure they get enough. A good rooster doesn't annoy his hens but struts around in front of them in a kind of rooster dance to see if they are interested in mating. Usually, in a small flock, one rooster is enough. It is never a great idea to have too many roosters as they can fight each other or stress out the hens.

Chicken can naturally usually live somewhere between 5-10 years.

YOU ARE THE WIND BENEATH MY WINGS!

AWESOME FACTS ABOUT CHICKENS & CHICKEN TALK

DID YOU KNOW?

- There is more that makes Silkie chickens unusual than just their fuzzy soft feathers. Silkies also have black skin underneath all that soft fluff. They also have black bones as well!

- You can put a chicken to sleep by covering its head with a towel.

- Having a few chickens is a great way to get fresh eggs, cut down on harmful yard and garden pests, use up otherwise wasted food, and move communities toward food stability.

- Hens still lay eggs whether there is a rooster around or not.

- Out of all birds, T-Rex dinosaur DNA is closest to the DNA of chickens!

- Chickens make over 24 different kinds of sounds to communicate with each other. Take a look at this quick guide for decoding the language of chickens.

CHICKEN TALK

Here are a few typical sounds and what they mean:

Tuck-Tuck-Tuck – This sound is a quick series of clucks that mean it's "*Time to eat!*" Often the rooster or others will make this sound when new food is put out to call the others to dinner time.

Brrrrrrrrrrrrrrrrh – This almost purring sound is made in a middle range (not too high or low) and is a constant trilled sound that may last for 3-4 seconds. It is a sound happy chickens make to signify all is well and good. A chicken that makes this sound is calm and relaxed.

Squawk! – This quick sound is loud and is similar to when you yell out "*Ahh!*" when startled. A chicken will say this sound if it is suddenly surprised or scared. Sometimes chickens peck each other to get them out of the way, and the pecked chicken may let out a quick squawk.

Buck-Buck-Buck-Buck-Bgock! – Sometimes chickens say this to tell others they need a little space because they are thinking of laying an egg. It is a lower, rhythmic sound. They may make this sound while in the nesting box or while getting ready to lay.

So, there you have it. The next time you are around chickens, see if you can interpret what some of their sounds mean!

And who knows, maybe you can even try making a few sounds yourself and have a chicken conversation with the hens.

THANKS FOR READING!

We hope you have learned more about chickens through this book. They really are great animals who deserve our respect and appreciation.

Did you know you can fight factory farming in a way that makes a difference? By choosing to buy organic or free-range meat and eggs (*or by buying meat and eggs from your local farmer's market*), you can support large and small farmers who are trying to raise chickens ethically and kindly.

Now, go spread the news about the amazing world of chickens!

THANK YOU!

Thank you for reading this book and for allowing us to share our love for chickens with you!

If you've enjoyed this book, please let us know by leaving a rating and a brief review wherever you made your purchase! This helps us spread the word to other readers!

Thank you for your time, and have an awesome day!

For more information, please visit:

www.animalreads.com

HOW LONG DO CHICKENS WORK?

Around the CLUCK!

© Copyright 2022 - All rights reserved Admore Publishing

ISBN: 978-3-96772-123-2

ISBN: 978-3-96772-124-9

Animal Reads at www.animalreads.com

The content contained within this book may not be reproduced, duplicated or transmitted without direct written permission from the author or the publisher.

Under no circumstances will any blame or legal responsibility be held against the publisher, or author, for any damages, reparation, or monetary loss due to the information contained within this book. Either directly or indirectly.

Published by Admore Publishing: Gotenstraße, Berlin, Germany

www.admorepublishing.com

www.ingramcontent.com/pod-product-compliance
Lightning Source LLC
LaVergne TN
LVHW020141080526
838202LV00048B/3984